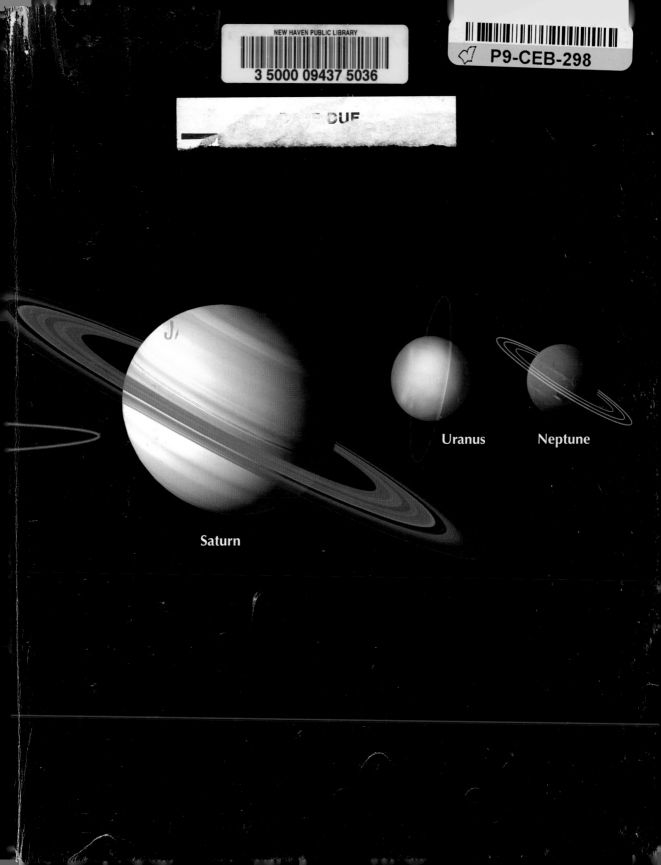

Earth and Earth's Moon

Editor in chief: Paul A. Kobasa
Supplementary Publications: Jeff De La Rosa, Lisa Kwon,
   Christine Sullivan, Scott Thomas, Marty Zwikel
Research: Mike Barr, Cheryl Graham, Jacqueline Jasek,
   Barbara Lightner, Andy Roberts, Loranne Shields
Graphics and Design: Kathy Creech, Sandra Dyrlund,
   Charlene Epple, Tom Evans, Brenda Tropinski
Permissions: Janet Peterson
Indexing: David Pofelski
Pre-Press and Manufacturing: Carma Fazio, Anne Fritzinger,
   Steven Hueppchen, Tina Ramirez
Writer: Lisa Klobuchar

First edition published 2006. Second edition published 2007.

WORLD BOOK and the GLOBE DEVICE are registered
trademarks or trademarks of World Book, Inc.

World Book, Inc.
233 N. Michigan Avenue
Chicago, IL 60601
U.S.A.

Library of Congress Cataloging-in-Publication Data
Earth and earth's moon -- 2nd ed.
    p. cm. -- (World book's solar system & space exploration
library)
    Summary: "Introduction to the Earth and Earth's moon,
providing to primary and intermediate grade students
information on their features and exploration. Includes fun facts
glossary, resource list and index"--Provided by publisher.
   Includes bibliographical references and index.
   ISBN-13: 978-0-7166-9512-7
   ISBN-10: 0-7166-9512-X
   1.   Earth--Juvenile literature. 2. Moon--Juvenile literature.
I. World Book, Inc.
QB631.4.E27 2007
525--dc22
                                    2006031509

ISBN-13 (set): 978-0-7166-9511-0
ISBN-10 (set): 0-7166-9511-1

Printed in the United States of America

1 2 3 4 5 6 7 8 09 08 07 06

**For information about other World Book publications,
visit our Web site at http://www.worldbook.com
or call 1-800-WORLDBK (967-5325).**

**For information about sales to schools and libraries,
call 1-800-975-3250 (United States);
1-800-837-5365 (Canada).**

Picture Acknowledgments: Front Cover: NASA; Back Cover: Jacques Descloitres, NASA/GSFC/MODIS
Land Rapid Response Team; NASA; © Calvin J. Hamilton; NASA; Inside Back Cover: © John Gleason,
Celestial Images.

© Corbis 31; © Calvin J. Hamilton 13, 37; © William K. Hartmann 51; NASA 1, 3, 11, 39, 41, 45, 53, 55,
59; NASA/John Frassanito and Associates 57; NASA/GSFC 20-21; Jacques Descloitres, NASA/GSFC/MODIS
Land Rapid Response Team, 17; NASA/JPL 35, 61; NASA/JPL-Caltech/R. Hurt (SSC-Caltech) 33;
NASA/JPL/NIMA 23; © Sally Bensusen, Photo Researchers 47; © Gregory G. Dimijian, Photo Researchers 27
(top); © Michael P. Gadomski, Photo Researchers 49 (top and bottom); © Rudiger Lehnen, Photo Researchers
27 (bottom).

Illustrations: Inside Front Cover: WORLD BOOK illustration by Steve Karp; WORLD BOOK
illustration 43; WORLD BOOK illustration by Oxford Illustrators 15; WORLD BOOK illustrations by
Paul Perreault 9, 19; WORLD BOOK illustration by Roberta Polfus 29; WORLD BOOK illustration by
Precision Graphics 7; WORLD BOOK map 25.

Astronomers use different kinds of photos to learn about objects in space—such as planets. Many photos
show an object's natural color. Other photos use false colors. Some false-color images show types of light
the human eye cannot normally see. Others have colors that were changed to highlight important features.
When appropriate, the captions in this book state whether a photo uses natural or false color.

WORLD BOOK'S

SOLAR SYSTEM & SPACE
EXPLORATION LIBRARY

Earth and
Earth's Moon

SECOND EDITION

World Book, Inc.
a Scott Fetzer company
Chicago

Contents

EARTH

If a word is printed in **bold letters that look like this,** that word's meaning is given in the glossary on page 63.

EARTH'S MOON

Where Is Earth?

The **planet** Earth is right under your feet. But Earth is also part of the **universe.** The universe is everything that exists anywhere in space and time.

A more specific way to explain Earth's location is to say that Earth is the third planet from the sun. Because the shape of Earth's **orbit** is oval, or **elliptical,** the planet's distance from the sun varies. On average, the distance is about 93 million miles (150 million kilometers).

Earth is one of the planets in our **solar system** that **astronomers** call the inner planets. The other inner planets are Mercury, Venus, and Mars. Earth's orbit is between the orbits of Venus and Mars. The planet that orbits closest to Earth is Venus. But, on average, Earth's orbit is about 26 million miles (41 million kilometers) farther from the sun than Venus's orbit is.

The orbit of Earth's outer neighbor, Mars, is about 49 million miles (78 million kilometers) farther from the sun than Earth's orbit is.

Planet Locator

Note: The size of the sun and planets and the distance between planets in this diagram are not to scale.

Neptune

Uranus

Saturn

Jupiter

Mars

Earth

Venus

Mercury

Sun

Earth's symbol (top left) and a diagram showing the planet's location in the solar system

How Big Is Earth?

Among the **planets** in our **solar system,** Earth is fifth largest in size. Jupiter is the largest planet, followed by Saturn, Uranus (*YUR uh nuhs* or *yu RAY nuhs),* and Neptune.

Earth's **diameter** at the **equator** is 7,926 miles (12,756 kilometers). But, if you could cut Earth in half and measure it straight through the center from the North Pole to the South Pole, the distance would be about 7,900 miles (12,700 kilometers). Earth bulges slightly at its equator, which is why its diameter is slightly larger at the equator than between the poles.

Earth is much smaller than the sun. The sun's diameter is about 109 times greater than Earth's diameter. But, Earth is about 4 times larger in diameter than its **moon.** If Earth's moon were the size of a tennis ball, Earth would be the size of a basketball.

The distance around Earth, measuring from the North Pole to the South Pole and back again, is 24,860 miles (40,010 kilometers). The distance around Earth along the equator is 24,900 miles (40,060 kilometers). Earth's total surface area is about 197 million square miles (510 million square kilometers).

An artist's drawing comparing the size of Jupiter and Earth

Earth's diameter
7,926 miles
(12,756 kilometers)

Jupiter's diameter
88,846 miles
(142,984 kilometers)

What Does Earth Look Like?

Earth is the only **planet** in our **solar system** with a lot of liquid water on its surface. The water makes Earth look blue when viewed from space. This is why Earth is sometimes called "the blue planet." Water covers about 71 percent of Earth's total surface area, or about 140 million square miles (362 million square kilometers). Clouds in Earth's **atmosphere** appear as white streaks against the blue.

Earth's continents, or land masses, appear brownish when viewed from space. About 29 percent of Earth's total surface area, or about 57 million square miles (148 million square kilometers), is land.

10

Earth in a
natural-color photo

What Makes Up Earth?

Much of Earth is made of rock. The inner **planets**—Mercury, Venus, Earth, and Mars—are grouped together not just because of their location in the **solar system,** but because they also are all made of rock.

The solid part of Earth has three layers: the **crust, mantle,** and **core.** Both the crust and mantle are made of rock. The crust is Earth's thin, cool, outer layer. The crust under the continents is mostly **granite** and similar rock. The crust under the oceans is much thinner and is mostly **basalt** (*buh SAWLT* or *BAS awlt*), which is a dense and dark volcanic rock. Beneath the crust, the mantle is a thick, hot, partially melted layer. Most of the mantle is made up of a group of minerals—called **silicates**—that consist of **silicon, oxygen,** and one or more metallic elements.

The core lies at the center of Earth. The core is made mostly of **iron** and **nickel.** The outer part of the core is liquid, and the inner part is solid.

The Interior of Earth

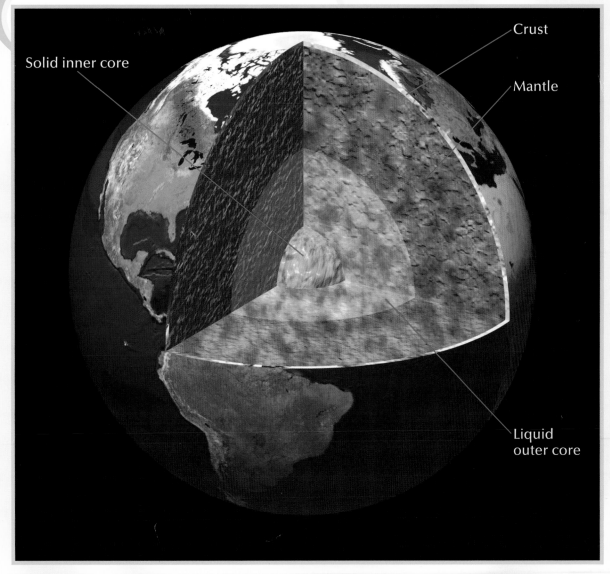

Solid inner core

Crust

Mantle

Liquid outer core

What Is Earth's Atmosphere Like?

Earth is wrapped in an envelope of air called the **atmosphere.** Earth's atmosphere is made up of four main layers.

Closest to Earth is the troposphere *(TROH puh sfihr)*. More than three-fourths of the atmosphere's gases are in the troposphere. These gases include mostly **nitrogen** and **oxygen.** Directly above the troposphere is the stratosphere *(STRAT uh sfihr or STRAY tuh sfihr)*. The upper troposphere and lower stratosphere contain a layer of gas called ozone *(OH zohn),* which blocks dangerous ultraviolet light from the sun. The other two layers of the atmosphere are the mesosphere *(MEHS uh sfihr or MEE suh sfihr)* and thermosphere *(THUR muh sfihr).*

The point at which the troposphere becomes the stratosphere is called the tropopause. Similarly, the stratopause is between the stratosphere and the mesosphere. And between the mesosphere and the thermosphere is the mesopause.

The Layers of the Atmosphere

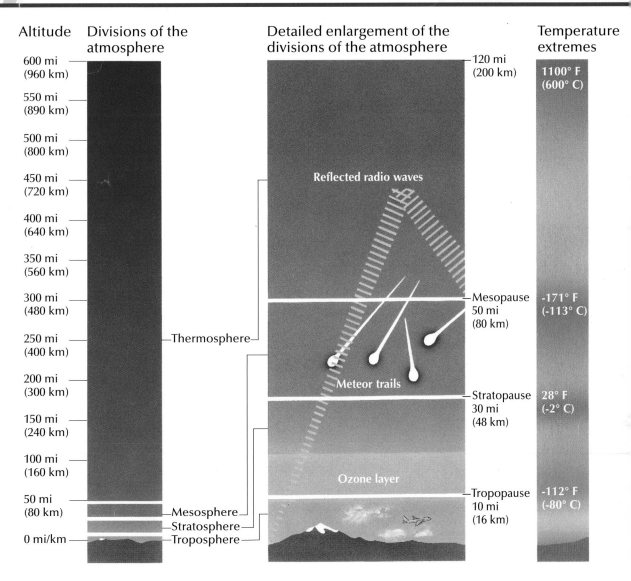

Altitude

600 mi (960 km)
550 mi (890 km)
500 mi (800 km)
450 mi (720 km)
400 mi (640 km)
350 mi (560 km)
300 mi (480 km)
250 mi (400 km)
200 mi (300 km)
150 mi (240 km)
100 mi (160 km)
50 mi (80 km)
0 mi/km

Divisions of the atmosphere

Thermosphere

Mesosphere
Stratosphere
Troposphere

Detailed enlargement of the divisions of the atmosphere

Reflected radio waves

Meteor trails

Ozone layer

120 mi (200 km)

Mesopause 50 mi (80 km)

Stratopause 30 mi (48 km)

Tropopause 10 mi (16 km)

Temperature extremes

1100° F (600° C)

-171° F (-113° C)

28° F (-2° C)

-112° F (-80° C)

What Is the Weather on Earth?

The cold temperatures at the North Pole or the hot temperatures in a desert may seem extreme to us. But, compared with other **planets** in our **solar system,** the weather on Earth is temperate—not too hot and not too cold. The weather on other planets is very extreme.

Nearly all of the weather that occurs on Earth—wind, storms, clouds, heat, or cold—happens in the layer of Earth's **atmosphere** called the troposphere (see page 14). That is because circulation, or movement of air, causes weather, and almost all of Earth's air is in the troposphere. Heat from the sun causes this air circulation. Warm air near the **equator** rises and flows toward Earth's poles. This air cools, returns to the surface, and finally flows back to the equator. This motion, combined with the rotation of Earth, moves heat and moisture around the planet, creating winds and weather patterns.

Space agencies and weather agencies have a number of **satellites** in the sky that watch Earth's surface at all times and keep track of weather conditions. These satellites help keep people safe by allowing scientists to predict typhoons and other kinds of dangerous storms.

A typhoon shown in a natural-color photo

What Are Earth's Orbit and Rotation Like?

Earth rotates (spins around) like a top on its **axis.** Earth takes 24 hours to spin completely around on its axis and come back to where the sun is in the same place in Earth's sky. This time period for Earth's rotation is called a solar **day.** At the **equator,** Earth rotates at about 1,000 miles (1,600 kilometers) per hour. (The speed decreases the closer you go to the poles, and at the poles the rotation speed is almost zero.)

Like all the other **planets** in our **solar system,** while Earth rotates on its axis, it also **orbits** around the sun. Earth's orbit is **elliptical,** or oval-shaped. This orbit lies on an imaginary flat surface around the sun called the orbital plane. Earth's trip around the sun takes 365 days 6 hours 9 minutes and 9.54 seconds. This is Earth's **year.**

During its year, Earth travels about 584 million miles (940 million kilometers). Earth travels at about 66,700 miles (107,000 kilometers) per hour, or 18.5 miles (30 kilometers) per second, as it moves along its orbit.

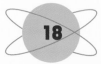

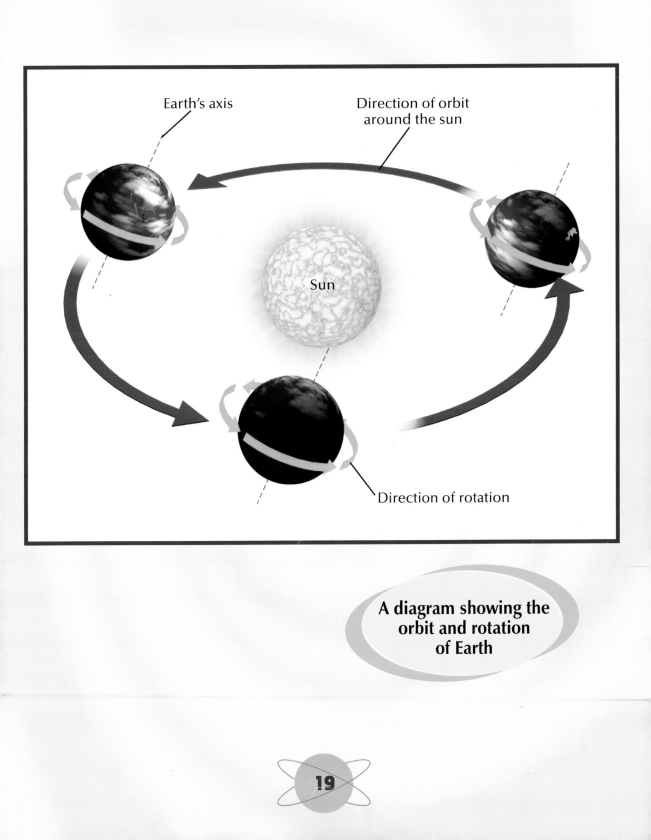

Earth's axis

Direction of orbit around the sun

Sun

Direction of rotation

A diagram showing the orbit and rotation of Earth

What Is Earth's Water Like?

   Water is made up of two molecules (basic units that make up matter) of **hydrogen** bonded with one molecule of **oxygen.** Water can be in different forms. It can be a solid—as ice—or a liquid. Or, water can be in a gas form, as vapor (steam).

   Water covers about three-fourths of Earth's surface. Because Earth has moderate temperatures, much of Earth's water is in liquid form. Most of this water—about 97 percent—is salty ocean water. Only about 3 percent is

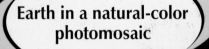

Earth in a natural-color photomosaic

fresh (unsalty) water. Much of Earth's fresh water is under the surface as ground water or frozen in icecaps around the **planet's** North and South poles. The rest of Earth's fresh water flows in rivers and streams and collects in large and small lakes.

Some of Earth's water evaporates and is carried into the **atmosphere.** This water eventually falls to Earth as rain or snow. Water that falls on land nourishes plants. Over time, this water can also wear down (erode) the land.

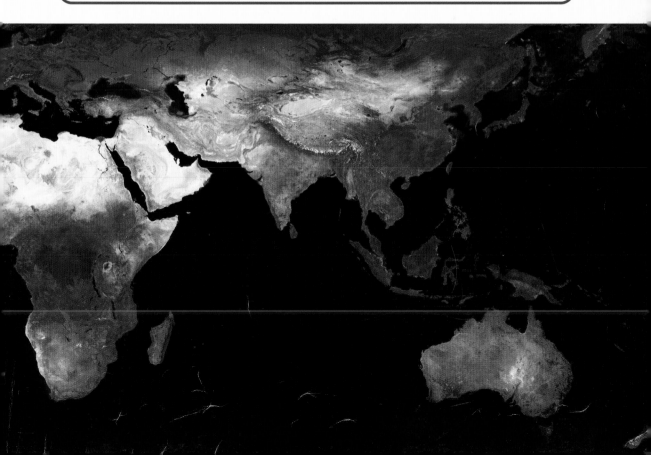

What Are Earth's Landforms?

Only about one-fourth of Earth's surface is land. Earth's landforms include mountains, valleys, and plains.

Mountains rise high above the surrounding land. Their peaks may be sharp or softly rounded. Earth's tallest mountains may be snow-covered the year around. Valleys are lowland areas between mountains or hills. Some valleys are narrow and deep, while others can be shallower and several miles or kilometers wide. Plains are large areas that are generally flat. Plains that receive a lot of rain are often covered with forests. Drier plains, on the other hand, often support grasses.

In 2000, the United States National Aeronautics and Space Administration (NASA) and the United States National Geospatial-Intelligence Agency (NGA) conducted the Shuttle Radar Topography Mission. The space shuttle Endeavour was launched to map Earth's landforms in 3-D (three dimensions) during this mission. Endeavour used radar (an electronic instrument used to detect and locate objects) to collect information for a topographic map of Earth. Topographic maps are detailed maps that show the heights of land features.

A 3-D map in false color, made by the Shuttle Radar Topography Mission

What Formed the Land?

Earth's mountains, valleys, and plains have formed over many millions of years. Many of them formed because of the movements of Earth's **crust.** Earth's crust is not one unbroken rocky "skin" over the **planet.** Instead, it is divided into a number of separate sections called tectonic *(tehk TON ihk)* plates. These plates fit together like giant puzzle pieces. The plates creep along very slowly. Today, these plates move about 4 inches (10 centimeters) a year. They may have moved even more slowly in the past. The plates float and move on top of rock in the Earth's **mantle** that is so hot it is acts like a thick liquid. As they move, the plates shape many of Earth's landforms.

Mountains and valleys often form at the places where tectonic plates meet. Some plates are pushing into one another. Where that happens, huge blocks of earth may be forced up into the air, forming tall mountains. Mountains also form where the edge of one plate plunges under the edge of another plate. Volcanoes and earthquakes are also common in these areas. Some plates are moving away from one another. Where plates move away from each other, deep rift valleys may open up. Long chains of volcanoes can form where molten (melted) rock wells up between the separating plates.

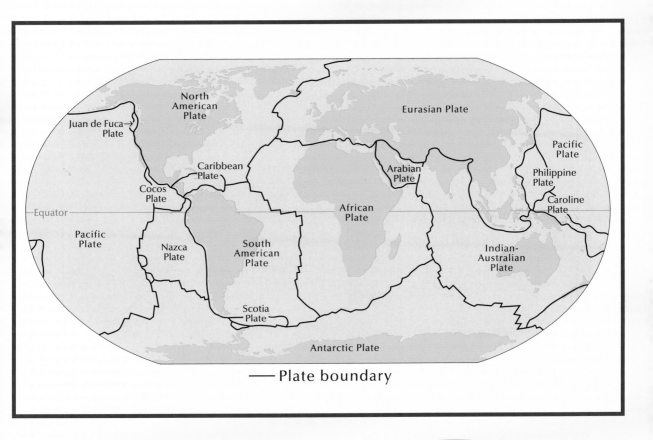

Plate boundary

A map showing the location of Earth's tectonic plates

How Does Earth Support Life?

Earth is the only place in the **universe** that is known to support life.

Most living things require moderate temperatures, which are provided by Earth's **atmosphere.** The atmosphere gives protection from harmful **radiation** from the sun, and it keeps plants warm enough for life. The atmosphere also provides **oxygen** that human beings and animals breathe.

Perhaps the most important factor that helps Earth to support life, however, is that the moderate temperatures allow for large amounts of liquid water on Earth's surface. All Earth's living things need liquid water to carry on their life processes.

The water on Earth's surface can absorb heat as well. This absorption helps keep Earth's temperature from becoming too hot or too cold. Ocean water stores much of the heat Earth gets from the sun.

Two-toed sloths hanging upside down in a rain forest

Some of the varied life forms on Earth

A green turtle on a coral reef

What Are Earth's Climate Zones and Seasons Like?

The amount of sunlight that falls on different parts of Earth is the main cause of differences in Earth's climate. The **equator** receives direct sunlight all year long. So, the temperature on the equator is always warm. Areas around the poles get the least amount of sunlight. These areas are cold. The areas in between have climates that are temperate—not too hot and not too cold.

Earth has seasons because its **axis** is tilted. As Earth **orbits** the sun, one half of Earth is tilted toward the sun for part of the year. This part of Earth has summer. At the same time the other half is tilted away from the sun. This part of Earth has winter.

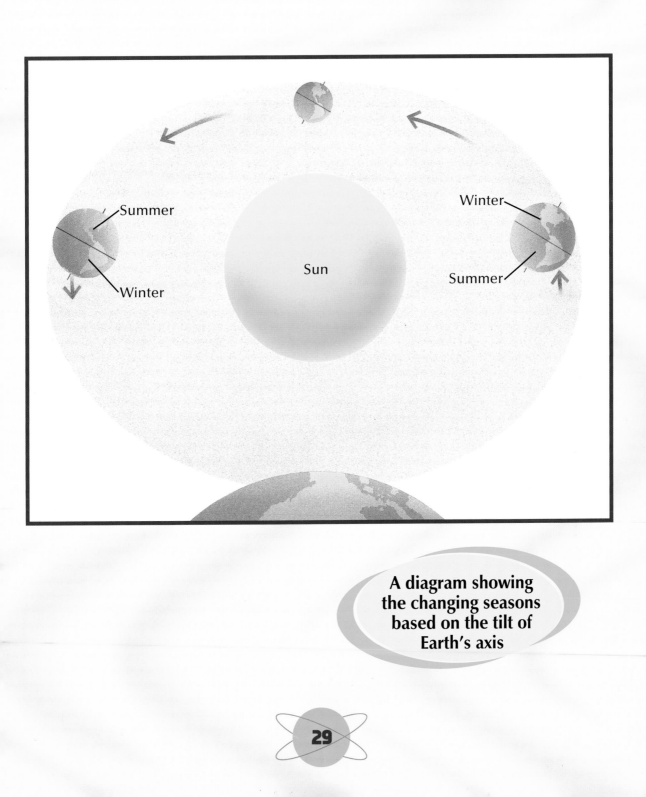

Summer

Winter

Sun

Winter

Summer

A diagram showing the changing seasons based on the tilt of Earth's axis

Where Is Earth's Moon?

Besides the sun, the **moon** is the most visible and familiar object in Earth's sky. Because of Earth's rotation from west to east, the moon seems to "rise" in the east. The moon moves high in the sky and "sets" in the west. Usually the moon shines at night. But at certain times it is visible during the day.

The moon **orbits** Earth, the third **planet** from the sun. It also travels along as Earth orbits the sun. The moon is Earth's closest neighbor in the **solar system** by far. It is, on average, about 239,000 miles (385,000 kilometers) from Earth.

The moon, visible in Earth's daytime sky

How Big Is the Moon?

Because the **moon** is very close to Earth, it seems about the same size as the sun and much larger than the **stars.** But the moon is really much smaller than the sun and stars. The **diameter** of the moon at its **equator** is about 2,159 miles (3,475 kilometers). The diameter of Earth at the equator is 7,926 miles (12,756 kilometers). This means the diameter of the moon is nearly four times smaller than Earth's diameter.

Compared with the moons of most other **planets,** though, Earth's moon is fairly large. For example, Deimos *(Dy mos),* one of the moons of Mars, has a diameter of 7.6 miles (12.2 kilometers). In fact, of the known moons in our solar system, only 29 have a **diameter** greater than 100 miles (160 kilometers).

An image comparing
the size of Earth with
its moon

What Does the Moon Look Like?

From the surface of Earth, the **moon** shines with a silvery glow in the night sky. With the unaided eye, the moon looks like a smooth globe with dark and light patches of gray on its surface.

With strong binoculars or a small telescope, the moon's surface features, such as **craters,** are easy to see. Features that appear as light patches of gray from afar are actually rough, cratered highlands called **terrae** *(TEHR ee).* The dark patches of gray are rocky lowlands called **maria** *(MAHR ee uh).* The maria are covered with **basalt**—a hard volcanic rock. Volcanoes on the moon erupted billions of years ago. The lava they produced then became solid, forming smooth rock. Maria look like large, dark bodies of water. In fact, *maria* is from the Latin word for seas.

The moon in a
false-color photo

What Makes Up the Moon?

The **moon** has an outer **crust** that is about 37 miles (60 kilometers) thick on the near side (the side that faces Earth) and about 50 miles (80 kilometers) thick on the far side (the side turned away from Earth). This outer crust is stiff and strong. Scientists do not know much about the moon's interior, but they believe it has a **mantle** of **iron** and **magnesium** and a **core** made mostly of iron. The core is probably about 500 miles (800 kilometers) across. The moon's surface is covered with a type of dark grayish soil, which is called **regolith** *(REHG uh lihth)*. Regolith consists of dustlike bits of rock. Tiny **meteorites** smashing into the moon over billions of years formed the regolith.

There are two main types of moon rocks, one is **basalt,** which is the hardened lava found in the **maria.** The other is breccia *(BREHCH ee uh* or *BREHSH ee uh)*, which is a type of scattered, crushed rock that is found mainly in the **terrae.**

The Interior of the Moon

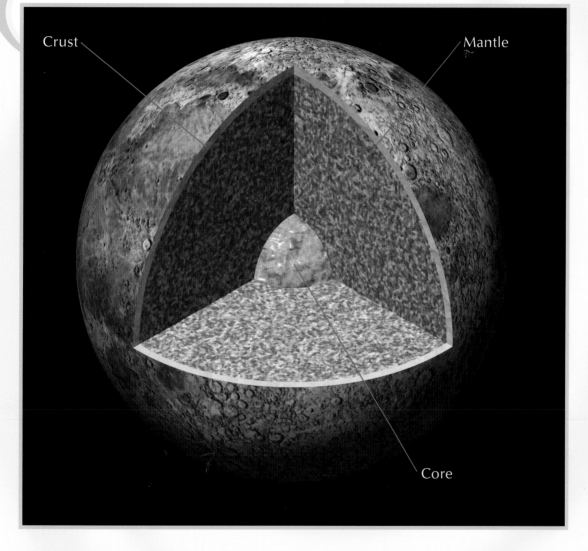

Crust

Mantle

Core

What Is the Surface of the Moon Like?

Probably the most familiar and spectacular of the **moon's** surface features are its millions of **craters.** Scientists guess that there are hundreds of thousands of craters on the moon that are more than half a mile (0.7 kilometer) wide. Millions more are at least 1 foot (30 centimeters) wide. The collision of **meteoroids, asteroids, comets,** and other space objects with the moon's surface over billions of years formed the craters.

Craters exist in many shapes and sizes. Older craters have softly rounded edges. Matter surrounds and fans out from the center of younger craters in a pattern resembling rays radiating from a light source. These rays are made up of matter that flew into the air when the crater was formed. Large craters sometimes have mountains in the middle. These mountains are made up of moon material that rebounded upward after the impact that caused the crater.

The moon's surface also has valleys and winding channels called **rilles** *(rihlz)*. Scientists now suspect that running lava formed the rilles some time ago.

A moon rock

How Does the Moon Compare with Earth?

You probably could not think of two objects in space that appear much more different than Earth and the **moon.** Earth is a lush, warm, watery **planet,** teeming with life. The moon, on the other hand, is a lifeless desert with extremely hot or extremely cold temperatures. The moon also has no **atmosphere,** so the sky would always look black from the surface of the moon. In addition, because the moon has no atmosphere, there is no wind. That means that footprints left on the moon's surface by astronauts should remain there unchanged for thousands of years.

Another difference between the moon and Earth would be the amount of **gravity** put forth by each object. The pull of gravity on the moon's surface is six times weaker than on Earth's surface. A boy or girl who weighs 90 pounds on Earth would weigh only 15 pounds on the moon. The reason for this is that the moon's **mass** is about 81 times smaller than Earth's mass.

A footprint made by an
astronaut on the moon

What Are the Orbit and Rotation of the Moon Like?

The **moon** travels in its **orbit** around Earth at about 2,300 miles (3,700 kilometers) per hour. Together, Earth and the moon orbit the sun. At the same time, both the Earth and the moon rotate (spin around) on their **axes.**

The moon has an interesting property—its rotation period and orbital period around Earth are close to the same, about 27 ⅓ days. This means that the moon takes the same amount of time to spin once on its axis as it takes to travel once around Earth. For this reason, only one side of the moon—the side called the near side— is visible from Earth. The other side—the far side— is always turned away from Earth.

Also, since the moon's rotation is so much slower than Earth's, one **day** on the moon lasts about 30 Earth days. That is the time it takes the moon to rotate one time on its axis and come back to the same position relative to the sun.

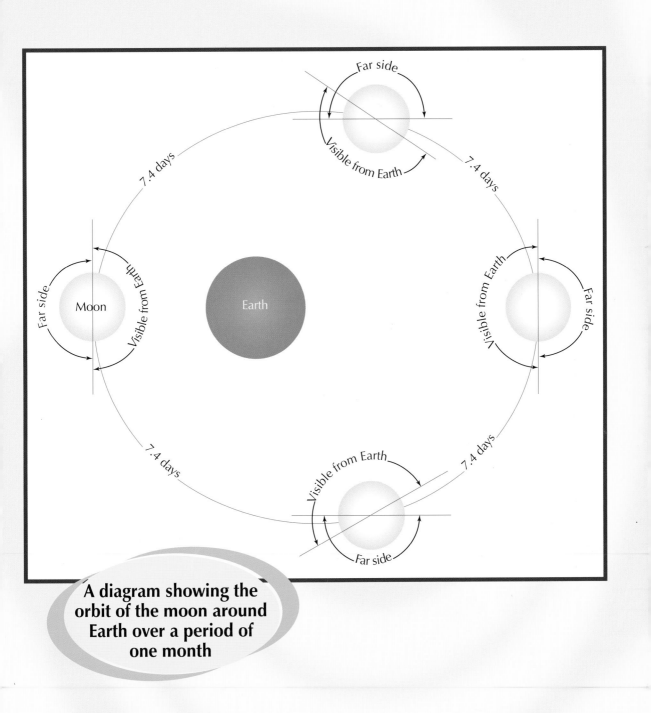

A diagram showing the orbit of the moon around Earth over a period of one month

Why Does the Moon Appear to Change Shape?

You've probably noticed that the **moon** looks a little bit different every night. One night, it will be completely dark and not visible at all. A couple nights later, it will appear again as a thin sliver shaped like a backward C. As the days pass, more and more of the moon becomes visible. Finally, after about two weeks, it is a full moon— a bright, round ball in the sky.

These different shapes are called **phases** of the moon. The moon's phases happen as a result of the moon's **orbit** around Earth and the orbit of the moon and Earth around the sun. When the moon is on the same side of Earth as the sun, the moon is not visible from Earth. This is called a new moon. When Earth is between the moon and the sun, one whole side of the moon is visible. This is called a full moon.

As the moon changes from a new moon to a full moon, it is said to be waxing. As the moon changes from full to new, it is waning. When the moon looks nearly full, that is a gibbous (GIHB uhs) moon. When it is shaped like a C or a backward C, that is a crescent moon.

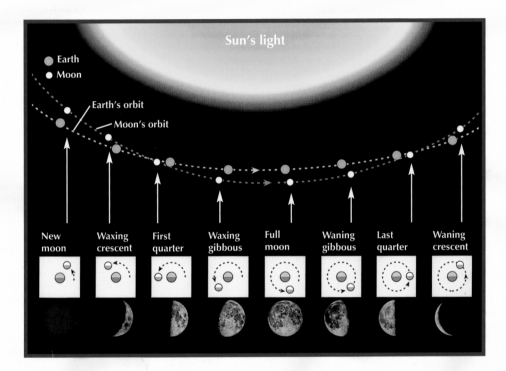

Sun's light

Earth
Moon

Earth's orbit
Moon's orbit

| New moon | Waxing crescent | First quarter | Waxing gibbous | Full moon | Waning gibbous | Last quarter | Waning crescent |

A diagram showing the phases of the moon

How Does the Moon Make the Sun Disappear?

About twice a year, somewhere on Earth, people are treated to the sight of the **moon** blocking the light from the sun. This special event is called a solar **eclipse.** In a total solar eclipse, the sun disappears completely, with only a glowing halo of light shining around the moon to show where the sun is.

A solar eclipse is a special kind of new moon. It happens when the sun, moon, and Earth line up in a straight line. When this happens, the moon, for a short time, blocks the light from the sun and throws a shadow on Earth.

Total eclipses are visible only in the path of totality, the area where the moon's darkest shadow falls on Earth. The path of totality is never wider than about 170 miles (274 kilometers). People who are outside but near the path of totality might see a partial solar eclipse, meaning the moon does not completely cover the solar disc when the eclipse is seen from their perspective. Others farther from the path of totality will not see any effect of the eclipse at all.

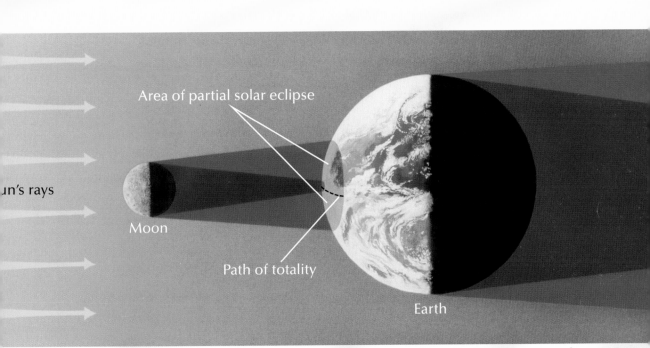

Area of partial solar eclipse

Sun's rays

Moon

Path of totality

Earth

**A diagram showing a
solar eclipse**

How Does the Moon Affect Earth's Oceans?

If you have ever spent time at the seashore, you have probably noticed how the water level rises and falls throughout the day. The tides cause these changes. And, the force of **gravity** between the **moon** and Earth is largely responsible for the tides.

Gravity is the force of attraction that acts between objects. The force of attraction is greater when the distance between the objects is shorter. On the side of Earth that faces the moon, the gravitational force of the moon is slightly stronger. It pulls on the oceans and causes the ocean water to bulge, or rise, in a high tide. Another high tide takes place at the same time on the opposite side of Earth, where the gravitational force of the moon is slightly weaker. The force is weak because that side of Earth is farther from the moon. On the sides of Earth at right angles to where the moon is, the water is at its lowest. On these two sides of Earth, there is low tide.

The force of the sun's gravity plays a much weaker role in determining the height of the tides.

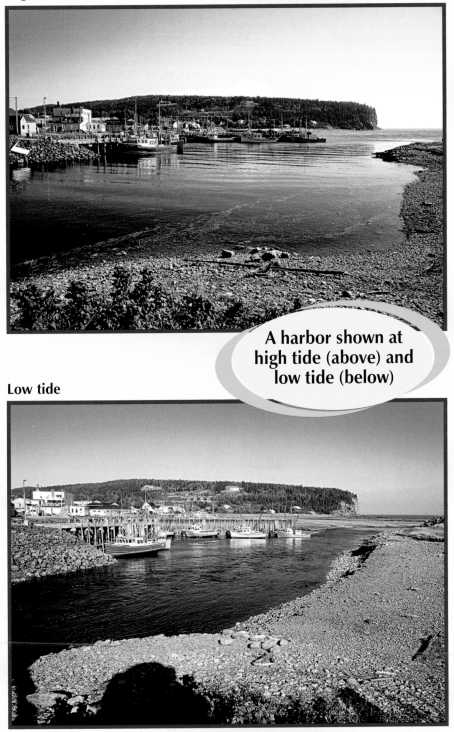

Low tide

A harbor shown at high tide (above) and low tide (below)

How Old Is the Moon?

Comparing **moon** rocks to Earth rocks has led most scientists to believe that the moon was formed when a huge object—about the size of the **planet** Mars—smashed into Earth. Scientists believe this event happened about 4.6 billion years ago.

When this huge object struck Earth, a cloud of material came off of our planet's surface and began **orbiting** around Earth. Over time, the cloud cooled and shrank into a ring of small, solid bodies. Eventually these small bodies gathered together, forming the moon.

As the small bodies collided and stuck together, they released a huge amount of heat. The new moon was probably covered in an ocean of melted rock. This melted rock eventually cooled and hardened. As the moon's **crust** became solid, many **asteroids** struck its surface. Some of the collisions between the moon and these asteroids were so powerful that they nearly broke the moon into pieces.

An artist's conception of a collision with Earth that may have formed Earth's moon

When Did People First Explore the Moon?

The Soviet Union—a large and powerful Communist country that existed from 1922 to 1991—sent the first space **probe** to the **moon.** The probe, called Luna 1, passed near the moon in January 1959. The first U.S. lunar probe was Pioneer 4, sent in March 1959. Luna 2 became the first probe to crash into the moon's surface in September 1959. In October 1959, Luna 3 photographed the far side of the moon—the side that faces away from Earth. It was the first time people could see what that side of the moon looked like.

In the mid-1960's, a number of U.S. and Soviet probes **orbited** and also made successful landings on the moon. These probes sent back pictures of the moon's surface and returned samples of the moon's soil. Many of these probes provided valuable information that allowed astronauts from the United States to land on the moon in 1969.

The far side of the moon, as captured by Luna 3, and the surface of the moon captured by the Lunar Orbiter 2 (inset)

How Did People Travel to the Moon?

In 1961, United States President John F. Kennedy set a goal to send astronauts to the **moon** before the end of the 1960's. This goal was met. NASA engineers working on the project, which was called Apollo, designed a spacecraft that would take the astronauts to the moon and land them on the surface. In December 1968, astronauts from the Apollo 8 mission became the first to **orbit** the moon.

The Apollo 11 mission successfully landed astronauts on the moon. On July 20, 1969, two astronauts, Neil A. Armstrong and Buzz Aldrin, stepped out of the lunar module (landing craft) and onto the moon's surface. Neil Armstrong was the first to set foot on the moon. His first words as he stepped on the surface were, "That's one small step for a man, one giant leap for mankind." Five more Apollo missions landed astronauts on the moon after Apollo 11.

Buzz Aldrin walks on the surface of the moon (left) and Apollo 11 lifts off (below)

Will People Return to the Moon?

In 2004, United States President George W. Bush set a goal of American astronauts returning to the **moon** by 2020. One important reason the U.S. government wants to return to the moon is to prepare astronauts for an even bigger mission—landing on Mars.

To prepare for future moon missions, NASA plans to launch the Lunar Orbiter Laser Altimeter (LOLA) in 2008. LOLA will create three-dimensional maps of the moon's surface. Such maps will enable scientists to choose good sites for future landing and exploration.

Soon after, NASA plans to launch several robotic missions to test equipment and help scout for the best locations to set up future space stations. The astronauts will use this information to plan for piloted missions to the moon and beyond. Astronauts could explore the surrounding area and conduct experiments from these space stations. The stations might even be enlarged into permanent moon colonies one day.

An artist's conception
of an exploration
spacecraft orbiting
the moon

What Could We Learn from Living on the Moon?

The **moon's** surface is similar in some ways to the surface of Mars. Both surfaces are dry, cold, and covered with dust. One of the most important things moon colonists might learn is how to live in such a dusty environment. They might learn how to deal with the dust that clings to their suits and all their equipment. Maybe they would also test modes of transportation, living quarters, sources of power, research tools, and other equipment that might apply to living on Mars.

Moon colonists might also experiment with ways of getting water from the ice in the moon's **regolith.** This water could be used for drinking. Perhaps astronauts would try to obtain **hydrogen** from the water on the moon and use it as rocket fuel. All the things that moon colonists might learn by living and working on the moon may help them to do the same on Mars.

An artist's conception of colonists on the moon

Could There Be Life on the Moon?

As far as anyone has been able to tell, there is no life as we know it on the **moon.** The moon lacks almost all the things needed by the life forms we are familiar with on Earth. These items needed to sustain life include (for many kinds of beings at least) liquid water and comfortable temperatures.

However, we now know that the moon has at least a little bit of ice. Two U.S. space **probes,** the Clementine in 1994 and the Lunar Prospector in 1998, found strong evidence of ice on the moon. The ice was found in **craters** at the moon's north and south poles, where the least amount of sunlight falls. Scientists believe that the ice was brought to the moon when a **comet** crashed into it 2 to 3 billion years ago. Could this mean that some form of life might be possible on the moon after all? Right now, scientists do not know for sure.

The south polar region of the moon in a black-and-white photo taken by the Clementine probe

★ Ninety percent of all the volcanic activity on Earth happens in Earth's oceans.

★ The highest point on Earth is Mount Everest, but when the Hawaiian volcano Mauna Kea is measured from the seafloor to its top, Mauna Kea is taller.

★ When the **probe** Lunar Prospector crashed into the **moon** at the end of its mission in 1999, it carried an ounce of ashes. The ashes were part of the cremated (burned) remains of the American geologist and **comet**-hunter Eugene Shoemaker, who had died in 1997. His fellow scientists sent his remains to the moon as a tribute to his life's work and his dream of going to the moon.

★ Many communities throughout the United States—and a few in other countries—are growing trees that sprouted from seeds that **orbited** the moon. Astronaut Stuart Roosa carried more than 400 seeds, gathered from loblolly pine, sycamore, sweet gum, redwood, and Douglas-fir trees, into orbit around the moon during the Apollo 14 mission in 1971. When he returned to Earth, scientists planted the seeds. The seeds sprouted, and the seedlings were distributed to be planted for the celebrations honoring the 200th anniversary of the United States in 1976. Many of these trees are alive today.

Glossary

asteroid A small body made of rock, carbon, or metal that orbits the sun. Most asteroids are between the orbits of Mars and Jupiter.

astronomer A scientist who studies stars and planets.

atmosphere The mass of gases that surrounds a planet.

axis In planets, the imaginary line about which the planet seems to turn, or rotate. (The axis of Earth is an imaginary line through the North Pole and the South Pole.)

basalt A hard, dark volcanic rock.

comet A small body made of dirt and ice that orbits the sun.

core The center part of the inside of a planet or moon.

crater A bowl-shaped depression on the surface of a moon or planet.

crust The solid, outer layer of a planet or moon.

day The time it takes a planet to rotate (spin) once around its axis and come back to the same position in relation to the sun.

diameter The distance of a straight line through the middle of a circle or anything shaped like a ball.

eclipse An event that happens when the shadow of one object in space falls on another object, or when one object moves in front of another to block its light.

elliptical Having the shape of an ellipse, which is like an oval or flattened circle.

equator An imaginary circle around the middle of a planet.

granite A hard, coarse-grained rock.

gravity The effect of a force of attraction that acts between all objects because of their mass (that is, the amount of matter the objects have).

hydrogen The most abundant chemical element in the universe.

iron A metallic chemical element.

magnesium A very light, metallic chemical element.

mantle The area of a planet or moon between the crust and the core.

maria Broad, flat, dark areas on the moon.

mass The amount of matter a thing contains.

meteorite A mass of stone or metal from outer space that has reached the surface of a planet without burning up in that planet's atmosphere.

meteoroid A small object, believed to be the remains of a disintegrated comet, which travels through space.

moon A smaller body that orbits a planet.

nickel A metallic chemical element.

nitrogen A nonmetallic chemical element.

orbit The path that a smaller body takes around a larger body, for instance, the path that a planet takes around the sun. Also, to travel in an orbit.

oxygen A nonmetallic chemical element.

phase The shape of the moon or of a planet as it is seen at a particular time.

planet A large, round body in space that orbits a star. A planet must have sufficient gravitational pull to clear other objects from the area of its orbit.

probe An unpiloted device sent to explore space. Most probes send data (information) from space.

radiation Energy given off in the form of waves or small particles of matter.

regolith The layer of soil and loose rock fragments overlying solid rock.

rille A snakelike channel on the moon. These channels wind across many areas of the moon's maria.

satellite An artificial satellite is an object built by people and launched into space, where it continuously orbits Earth or some other body.

silicate A group of minerals that contain silicon, oxygen, and one or more metallic elements. Silicates make up about 95 percent of Earth's crust.

silicon A nonmetallic chemical element found only combined with other elements, chiefly with oxygen in silica.

solar system A group of bodies in space made up of a star and the planets and other objects orbiting around that star.

star A huge, shining ball in space that produces a tremendous amount of light and other forms of energy.

terra Part of the moon's surface that is not one of the maria (plural, terrae).

universe Everything that exists anywhere in space and time.

year The time it takes a planet to complete one orbit around the sun.

Index

For more information about Earth and Earth's moon, try these resources:

The Near Planets, by Robin Kerrod, Raintree, 2002

Earth:

Earth, by John Farndon, DK Concise Encyclopedias, 2002

Earth: Our Planet in Space, by Seymour Simon, Simon &
    Schuster Children's Publishing, 2003

Moon:

Apollo Moonwalks, by Gregory Vogt, Enslow, 2000

The Moon, by Seymour Simon, Simon & Schuster
    Children's Publishing, 2003

Earth:

http://walrus.wr.usgs.gov/ask-a-geologist/

http://www.earth.nasa.gov/flash_top.html

http://www.jpl.nasa.gov/earth/

Moon:

http://astrogeology.usgs.gov/SolarSystem/Earth/Moon/

http://nssdc.gsfc.nasa.gov/planetary/lunar/apollo_25th.html

http://nssdc.gsfc.nasa.gov/planetary/planets/moonpage.html